YOU CHOOSE

BRAVE ESCAPES FROM STALAG LUFT I

INTERACTIVE WORLD WAR II MISSIONS

by Eric Braun

CAPSTONE PRESS
a capstone imprint

Published by Capstone Press, an imprint of Capstone
1710 Roe Crest Drive, North Mankato, Minnesota 56003
capstonepub.com

Library of Congress Cataloging-in-Publication Data
is available on the Library of Congress website.

ISBN: 9798875244537 (hardcover)
ISBN: 9798875244506 (paperback)
ISBN: 9798875244513 (ebook PDF)

Summary: Stalag Luft I was a German prison camp that held Allied airmen during World War II. During its operation, many prisoners attempted daring escapes. And at the end of the war, Allied forces conducted Operation Revival to evacuate everyone still held captive. Would you rather try your luck as a prisoner tunneling to freedom or take your chances as an officer involved in the high-stakes rescue plan? Now is your chance to do both—and more! In this interactive adventure, YOU CHOOSE the paths that will lead you and others to freedom . . . or spell your doom!

Editorial Credits
Designer: Bobbie Nuytten; Media Researcher: Svetlana Zhurkin;
Production Specialist: Katy LaVigne

Image Credits
Alamy: De Luan, 85, piemags/ww2archive, 37; Associated Press: 4; DVIDS: Courtesy of Linda Moore/Photo by Staff Sgt. Ryan Campbell, 55, 82, Courtesy of Master Sgt. Matthew Carey/Photo by Senior Airman Yash Rojas, 107, Courtesy of Richard Burdette/Photo by Tech. Sgt. Carlos Trevino, 79; Getty Images: Hulton Archive, 10, 17, Maurizio Fabbroni, 28; NARA: U.S. Air Force, 43, 94, 108 (bottom); Newscom: Everett Collection, 102; Shutterstock: alphaspirit, 34, Aneta Jungerova, 59, BlueBarronPhoto, 98, 108 (middle), Buch and Bee (airplane emblem), 5 and throughout, Czerep rubaszny, 6–7 (base map), ddimitris, 47, Deutschland Abgelichtet, 23, 67, George Trumpeter, cover (bottom), jollys_art (old paper), cover and throughout, Oleg Golovnev, 74, Oleksii Konchenko, 8, 12, 44, 72, 100, Pablo Caridad (paper file), 1 and throughout, ranchorunner, cover (top), Tomas Picka, 14, Valentin Agapov (folder), back cover and throughout; SuperStock: Wide World Photo/Sydney Morning Herald, 105, World History Archive/Image Asset Management, 88

Printed and bound in China. 6461

TABLE OF CONTENTS

American airmen at Stalag Luft I in May of 1945

ABOUT YOUR ADVENTURE

YOU are an Allied airman during World War II (1939–1945), and the winds of war have delivered you to a moment you never saw coming. You might be a prisoner trying to escape from Stalag Luft I, a German prison camp near the Baltic Sea. Or you could be taking part in a daring rescue mission to evacuate prisoners from that camp at the end of the war.

Whichever fate you face, YOU CHOOSE the paths that will determine your destiny. If you choose wisely, you and others may finally find a way to freedom. But one wrong choice could also lead to total failure. Will your decisions help you succeed or spell your doom?

Turn the page to begin your adventure.

STALAG LUFT I AND OPERATION REVIVAL

UNITED KINGDOM
Stalag Luft I
Barth
Baltic Sea
GERMANY
POLAND
Le Havre
Camp Lucky Strike
FRANCE

The Prison Camp:

Stalag Luft I was a German prison camp located right outside the seaside city of Barth, Germany. During the early years of World War II, it mainly held British airmen. But by 1943, American prisoners started being transferred to the prison as well. As the war came to an end, about 9,000 prisoners were being held at the camp.

The Mission:

Operation Revival was an Allied rescue mission that took place from May 12–14, 1945. During the mission, more than 450 bomber flights liberated nearly 9,000 prisoners from Stalag Luft I. More than 7,500 prisoners were American and about 1,350 were British.

The bombers used during Operation Revival left from American air bases in England and flew single file to an air strip just outside of Barth, Germany. Most of the liberated prisoners were brought to the French port of Le Havre. From there, the Americans went to Camp Lucky Strike to await their final trip home. Meanwhile, the British went home from Le Havre.

SOVIET UNION

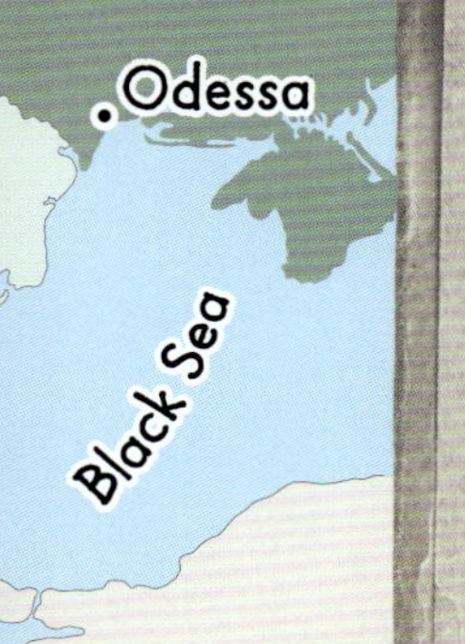

Key Terms

Allies—the United Kingdom, the United States, the Soviet Union, China, and France

Gestapo—the secret police of Nazi Germany

Kriegies—a name Allied prisoners called themselves; it was based on a German word for "prisoner of war"

Nazi—a member of a political party led by Adolf Hitler; the Nazis ruled Germany from 1933 to 1945

Soviet Union—a former federation of 15 republics that included Russia, Ukraine, and other nations of eastern Europe and northern Asia

Chapter 1

NOTORIOUS PRISON CAMPS

YOU are an airman on the side of the Allies in World War II, and you have a strong record as a pilot. You've never been shot down or caught. That's good, because you do not want to end up in a German prison camp.

You've heard a lot about these camps and how prisoners of war (POWs) are treated in them. Conditions can be brutal, with overcrowded barracks and meager rations. Guards mostly treat prisoners well enough, but you have heard stories about exceptions. Some guards are violent, and in some camps the Nazi Schutzstaffel, or SS, are involved. The SS is a paramilitary group known for its cruelty. Certainly, some prisoners are killed in German POW camps.

The German Air Force ran several Stalag Luft camps in Germany and occupied territories in Europe.

The camps are spread all over Germany. Stalags are the most common. They are for enlisted men. Oflag camps are specifically for officers. Arbeitslagers are labor camps where prisoners are sent to work in factories. As an airman, you worry most about Stalag Luft camps. They are run by German airmen and hold Allied airmen.

You've also heard about numerous escape attempts. Stories include soldiers digging tunnels, forging documents, making disguises, bribing guards, and more.

These stories lead you to imagine what it would be like in a POW camp. How would you hold up? Would you be able to trust the other prisoners? The stories of escape are inspiring but also worrisome. Most attempts fail, after all. Punishment for trying to escape could mean long sentences in solitary confinement and even execution.

You shiver at the thought, now more certain than ever that you'd rather not experience a German POW camp for yourself. But little do you know, the winds of fate are shifting. Soon, you will be pushed toward Stalag Luft I. It is a POW camp for airmen near the German city of Barth.

To be a British fighter pilot early in the war, turn to page 13.

To be an American pilot late in the war, turn to page 45.

To be an American officer after Germany's surrender, turn to page 73.

Chapter 2

EARLY DAYS IN CAMP

The day is gray and gloomy as you fly through the clouds in your one-seat Spitfire fighter plane. The other planes in your squadron fly in formation alongside you. Somewhere in the air behind you flies a squadron of bombers. Your mission is to protect them so they can bomb a German air strip near the Baltic Sea.

Suddenly, gunfire fills the air as a squad of German fighters approaches. Your friend Bonnell opens fire and hits a German plane. It trails black smoke as it falls from the sky.

"Nice shot, mate!" you call over the radio.

But there's no time for chit-chat. The Germans fire on you, and you climb above the clouds to avoid them. Then you dive, squeezing the trigger on your machine gun.

Turn the page.

A Spitfire fighter plane downing a German plane

Another hit! The enemy fighters peel off and begin a retreat. You adjust your oxygen mask and try to enjoy the quiet while you have it. You know it won't last.

Finally, the air strip is in view. It looks like the bombers will get their chance. Once again, you hear gunfire as German planes reappear. You also hear louder shots as anti-aircraft guns fire from the ground near the air strip.

"Aaah!" It's Bonnell in your ear on the radio. You look to the north and see his plane in flames. In a matter of seconds, it explodes.

A split second later, a sinister *thunk!* echoes through your own plane. Your plane plummets downward.

You manage to land on the surface of the Baltic Sea. You put on your life vest and inflate your dinghy just as your plane sinks. Only now do you realize that your leg is bleeding. You've been shot.

You float helplessly in the dinghy for more than an hour before a German patrol boat picks you up. Though they are the enemy, your leg hurts so badly, and you're so cold, you are almost glad to see them. They bring you to a hospital, where your leg is treated.

A week later you're transferred to Stalag Luft I. The prison camp is surrounded by a double barbed-wire fence. The space between the fences is filled with coiled barbed wire three feet high. Soldiers with machine guns and search lights are stationed in towers.

Turn the page.

You are assigned to a barracks room with nine other men, all members of the Royal Air Force (RAF) like you. When they question you about how the war is going, you tell them what you know. Later that night, after lights out, one of the prisoners whispers your name.

"Yeah?" you answer.

"I need your help," he says. He has collected dozens of tinfoil wrappers from cigarette packages, which he tells you can be useful for an escape.

"Why don't you keep them?" you ask.

"The guards are onto me," he says.

If you are caught with the tinfoil, you could be punished with solitary confinement or worse. On the other hand, you would like to make friends with these other men. Perhaps you all can escape together.

To hide the tinfoil for him, go to page 17.

To turn him down, turn to page 19.

British airmen in their barracks at a Stalag Luft camp

“Hand them over,” you say.

You hear shuffling noises in the dark. A moment later, the man slips a small cloth sack into your hand.

“Name’s Chinook,” he whispers. “I appreciate your help.”

You slip out of bed and run your hands along your mattress. It’s an old, beaten-up thing, and it doesn’t take long to find a tear. You shove the sack deep inside and then climb back into bed.

Turn the page.

That night you dream of your friend Bonnell. His bright smile and big laugh play in your mind.

The next morning, Chinook comes up to you in the recreation yard.

"We're digging a tunnel," he whispers. "Want to join us?"

An escape plan! The hairs on your neck stand up. The danger is sky high. The tunnel could collapse, crushing or suffocating whoever is in it. Even worse, you could get caught. Prisoners caught trying to escape are punished severely. Maybe you should wait until you understand how things work around here a little better.

To join the escape effort, turn to page 21.

To turn him down, at least for now, turn to page 22.

"Sorry, mate, I'll pass," you say.

You don't want to take the chance of getting caught with contraband so early in your stay here. Who knows what the guards would do to you?

The man curses at you, but he doesn't ask again.

A couple weeks later, you are lying in bed when a loud air raid siren suddenly goes off. Then all the lights in camp go out. This protects the camp and nearby town of Barth from being hit by Allied bombers. Now it's pitch black in camp.

Just beneath the wail of the siren you hear another sound in the dark. A couple men in your room are scurrying around.

"What's going on?" someone says.

"Escape," says one of the men. "Now."

"How?" you ask.

Turn the page.

"There's no moon and no lights," says one of the men, pulling on his jacket. "It's too dark for them to see us."

And with that, he and a few other guys simply climb out the window and are gone.

You think about the tall fences topped with barbed wire and the mounds of coiled barbed wire between them. Can you get across all that? The men seem to think they can. Do they have a plan for what to do if they get out? It all seems rash and risky. Of course, you may never get another chance to get away.

To join them, turn to page 24.

To play it safe and stay put, turn to page 27.

You figure Chinook must have a plan, and you do not want to spend one more day here than you have to. So, you give him a nod—a subtle signal that you are in.

That night in the barracks, you learn all about the secret plan. They need help in two areas—someone to dig the tunnel and someone to sew clothing to wear after you get out.

Tunneling sounds very scary and dangerous. But sewing clothes means you'll have to hide your sewing supplies and the clothing you make. Getting caught with those things would also be very bad.

To dig, turn to page 29.

To sew, turn to page 32.

You're still new here, and you want to learn the ropes before you get involved in something that might be dangerous.

"I need to lay low until I get the lay of the land," you say to Chinook. He shakes his head in disappointment and walks away.

One of the nice things about life in Stalag Luft I is that it is run by German airmen. It's true that they hate the Allied prisoners and would kill them if given a reason. But they also give you a certain amount of respect since you are in your country's air force.

That may be why they give you certain perks and freedoms. One of your favorites is going to the beach outside of camp now and then. One day, armed guards take you and your friends on one of these trips.

At the beach, you go swimming. You are floating on your back, thinking about flying again, when you hear laughter.

Baltic Sea coast near Barth, Germany

You glance back at shore. The guards are joking and fooling around. One is lying on his back, his rifle several feet away from him. Another has his back to the water. The third is facing you, but he is laughing and talking.

Nobody is paying attention. You might be able to dive underwater and swim far out to sea. You might be able to escape. You might also get shot. But the farther you swim, the harder it will be for them to hit you.

To try to swim away, turn to page 34.

To stay put, turn to page 36.

You climb out the window. The air raid siren is loud, covering the sounds you make. The darkness is complete. You run toward the fence feeling confident.

When you get there, you begin to climb. The man ahead of you cuts through the coiled barbed wire—he must have been hiding wire cutters. You can't believe it is this easy!

Before you know it, you're outside the camp, running into the woods. The other three men have forged papers, and they plan to head for Barth to get on a train. You aren't prepared with papers, but one of the men gives you some money and a crust of bread.

"It's all I can spare," he says.

You thank him and then run through the night. It's hard to make good time because of your injured leg, and you take frequent breaks. On the second night, you hear barking dogs. Before long, you are caught.

When you return to Stalag Luft I, you are put in a solitary cell for four days. Then you are returned to the barracks where a British officer named Dalton yells at you. He tells you that prisoners trying to flee must get approval from an escape committee. If your scheme is approved, help will be provided.

"Those other men had papers because they'd gone through the committee," Dalton barks at you. "But you went off without a plan and may have blown everyone's cover."

But Dalton isn't totally angry with you because you now have something he and the committee want. You've seen the area outside camp. And when you tell them everything you saw, they seem happy.

"There's a tunnel being dug from inside the incinerator near the sports field," Dalton says, speaking of the low building where trash is burned. "You can join us if you want."

Turn the page.

You eagerly agree and are given a job. You are to stand on the incinerator with other men, as if you are watching the soccer match in the field. But your real purpose is to block the view of the guards while another prisoner enters the incinerator to dig.

You do this for several days. Then one day, something goes wrong. While your friend is underground digging, a guard starts walking toward the incinerator. You might be able to signal the digger to get out in time. Or you could try to distract the guard.

To signal the digger, turn to page 38.

To distract the guard, turn to page 40.

You want to go, but there are too many unknowns. So, you stay put. The three men who climbed out do not come back that night. For a few days, you all wait nervously for news.

A week later, two of the men are recaptured and brought back. But the other never returns, and you're convinced he is free. You decide if you have a chance again, you'll take it.

Sure enough, there's another air raid a few weeks later. This time, you don't hesitate to climb out your window.

"I wouldn't do that if I were you," says Chinook from the window above you. He is one of the prisoners who got recaptured. But you don't listen. All you can think about is freedom.

You sprint across the yard to the fence. You leap onto it and begin climbing as fast as you can.

Turn the page.

Suddenly, a rifle shot rings out. You freeze. Terror fills your veins, and a sharp pain spreads out across your back. You look at your hands as your grip on the fence loosens. The darkness around you grows even darker, then all goes completely black as you fall.

THE END

To follow another path, turn to page 11.
To learn more about Stalag Luft I, turn to page 101.

Sewing would mean holding contraband full time until you escape. Tunneling sounds terrifying, but at least when you're *not* tunneling you are safe. You tell Chinook you will dig.

That night, he shows you some loose boards in the floor behind his bed. Beneath them is a crawl space. You grab the coal shovel for the stove, climb into the space, and crawl to the end of the building. There, you find the hole. It's barely big enough to fit your body. Your heart races, but you crawl into the tunnel with the shovel in front of you. When you reach the end, you scrape and dig at the earth in front of you.

After a few minutes, you must crawl backward to get some air. The tunnel is so narrow that fresh air can't circulate past your body.

Turn the page.

After a few days of this, you have an idea. You build an air pump using a fire bellows and a long tube of rolled-up wallpaper peeled from the barracks wall. You suspend the tube from the ceiling of the tunnel with wire so it reaches the end. Now, while you dig, Chinook pumps the bellows from the barracks so that fresh air travels down the line and into the tunnel in front of you. With this method, you can dig much longer and with more energy than before.

One day, a package arrives from the RAF with a board game in it. The Nazi guards inspect it, find nothing suspicious, and let you have it. But it's not just a game. A tiny map and some money is ingeniously tucked underneath the game board's surface. One of the game pieces also conceals a compass. These supplies will help you during your escape.

Finally, the night of the escape arrives. You and several other men wrap homemade Nazi uniforms into cloth sacks and crawl, one by one, through the tunnel. You emerge in a field beyond the camp fences and silently run into the woods. The moon hangs high in the sky, giving you just enough light to make your way. As you and your friends change into your new clothes, you can't help smiling. You just might make it home!

THE END

To follow another path, turn to page 11.
To learn more about Stalag Luft I, turn to page 101.

“I’ll sew clothes,” you tell him. The idea of crawling into a narrow tunnel horrifies you.

Over the next couple weeks, you work in the darkness after lights out. Your task is to sew clothing that will look like Nazi uniforms—at least from a distance.

One night, the guards come around with their dogs, and you hide your supplies carefully behind a loose board in the wall. They let the dogs into the crawl space below the floor of the barracks, but luckily nobody is digging at this time.

One of the dogs keeps sniffing around your bed. The guard handling the dog shines his flashlight all along the wall and notices the loose board. He pulls it open and finds your sewing equipment and the fake Nazi uniforms. You are thrown into a solitary cell as punishment for a week.

When you get out, you are subjected to daily searches. Suddenly, none of the other prisoners wants to be seen talking to you. The escape plan is also put on hold because searches become more frequent.

As the war goes on, other Allied men are marched from other prison camps to Stalag Luft I, including Americans for the first time. The camp is getting overcrowded, and food is low. Soon you get so sick, you aren't sure if you'll live to see the end of the war.

THE END

To follow another path, turn to page 11.
To learn more about Stalag Luft I, turn to page 101.

You figure you may never get such an opportunity again, so you decide to go for it. Without a word to any of your friends, you dive beneath the water and swim away from shore. You stay underwater until your lungs feel like they may burst. Then you surface just long enough to take two deep breaths and listen. You don't hear any yelling from shore, so you dive again.

The next time you come up, you hear gunfire. The guards are shooting at you! You take a deep breath and dive. You swim as hard and as far as you can. The gunshots sound faint down here. You stroke along the floor of the sea, but it's getting darker and hard to see what's ahead of you.

Suddenly, your head strikes a large rock. You try to keep swimming, but the pain makes you gasp and inhale a mouthful of seawater. You push for the surface, but your head is swimming with colors. You realize you are about to pass out. Most likely you will drown. But if you don't, you'll certainly be shot.

THE END

To follow another path, turn to page 11.
To learn more about Stalag Luft I, turn to page 101.

You're a strong swimmer, but you can't swim faster than bullets! You decide it's safer to go back to camp and keep working with the other prisoners on your escape plan.

The leader of the escape committee in your barracks tasks you with melting tinfoil to make Nazi buttons and ID badges. These will be sewn onto fake uniforms made from dyed bedsheets and other clothes. These disguises will help you pass as German soldiers after you get out.

At last, time for the tunnel escape arrives. You and the others in your group crawl through the narrow tunnel. You are in the middle of the line, pushing your bundled fake uniform ahead of you. Excitement courses through you like electricity. But just as the first man in your crew emerges from the tunnel up ahead, you hear a dog barking. Then you hear shouting.

A German guard crawling through a narrow tunnel that POWs dug to escape from Stalag Luft I

Your heart sinks. Your escape was timed to happen when the guard and his dog were usually on the opposite side of the compound. But he must have changed his routine. Or perhaps you mistimed it. Whatever the case, you are caught now.

THE END

To follow another path, turn to page 11.
To learn more about Stalag Luft I, turn to page 101.

You need to get the digger out before the guard gets any closer, so you climb down from the incinerator.

"Guard coming!" you whisper.

The man in the tunnel shimmies out feetfirst and emerges from the building just as the guard strolls past.

The guard pauses by your group. "Why is he covered in dirt?" he asks, pointing to your friend.

Then the guard peers inside the incinerator. He sees the tunnel opening and blows his whistle. Immediately, more guards show up.

When you get out of solitary confinement a week later, you learn that security is very high now. In fact, the German leader Adolph Hitler's SS troops are being called in to deal with prisoners who try to escape.

You know all about the SS. These elite fighters are cruel, torturous thugs and heartless killers. So, you decide to avoid getting involved with any more escape attempts.

More than a year goes by. By now, American POWs are joining the population at Stalag Luft I from other camps. Those camps are closing because the Allies are taking territory from the Germans.

It's clear the Allies are close to winning the war. But some prisoners worry the SS will start killing POWs because they have nothing to lose. These prisoners want to escape. On the other hand, if the war is about to end, you'll be freed soon enough anyway.

To try to escape again, turn to page 41.

To wait it out, turn to page 42.

Distracting the guard is the smartest way to go. As he walks closer, you turn your back and stick your finger down your throat. Instantly, you gag and throw up all over your shoes.

"What is this?" the guard yells. He calls over two more guards. They take you back to your barracks, but they are suspicious. They conduct daily searches of the room for the next few days. The tunnel digging is put on hold until the searches slow down.

Two weeks later, your patience pays off. You and the others begin digging inside the incinerator again. Soon, the tunnel reaches the athletic field outside of camp, and you make your escape. But you still have a long journey ahead as you make your way across the German landscape to safety.

THE END

To follow another path, turn to page 11.
To learn more about Stalag Luft I, turn to page 101.

Like some of the other prisoners, you are too anxious to simply wait. You are also worried about how the SS may treat you when Allied troops close in.

With three other men, you make a plan to tunnel out. Since the incinerator tunnel has been discovered, you dig your tunnel from inside the barracks.

With only four of you on the team, it's exhausting work. You are up late every night digging, moving dirt, or keeping watch.

One night, you fall asleep on watch and only wake up when you hear the guard's dogs barking at your barracks door. You rush to signal your friends under the floor, but it's too late. The SS grab all of you and line you up against the fence in the yard. You close your eyes and wait for the sound of the firing squad.

THE END

To follow another path, turn to page 11.
To learn more about Stalag Luft I, turn to page 101.

Why take chances with the end of the war in sight? You've already been here for years. Why not wait a little longer to be rescued?

Finally, you learn that Soviet soldiers are approaching the camp within days. In response, the camp's commandant orders everyone to evacuate. You'll be marching to another camp before the Soviets arrive.

But the American officer in charge of the prisoners, Colonel Zemke, has different ideas. He tells the camp's commandant that the prisoners will wait here for the Soviets instead. The German guards may have guns, Zemke explains, but there are thousands of prisoners who will arm themselves with knives and clubs.

"We will prevail," Zemke says.

The camp's commandant apparently agrees because he and his men flee that night.

Colonel Hubert Zemke was the highest-ranking officer and a respected leader at Stalag Luft I.

Now Zemke is in charge, and he has everyone put on white armbands stating their nationality in Russian. The Soviets arrive shortly thereafter. Over time, an air rescue is negotiated. It will not be long before you and all the other prisoners in Stalag Luft I are flying home.

THE END

To follow another path, turn to page 11.
To learn more about Stalag Luft I, turn to page 101.

Chapter 3

END IN SIGHT

You are an American fighter pilot who has been imprisoned in a German camp for more than a year. You and your fellow prisoners call yourselves Kriegies, which is short for a German word that means "prisoner of war."

Now it is late 1944, and some of your fellow Kriegies are losing hope that they'll ever get out of here. Then one day, something changes. The Nazi guards wake you early, tell you to gather your things, and line you up in the yard. They tell you everyone—including the guards—is leaving this camp for good.

You have heard rumors that Soviet forces are advancing on the Western Front—and it turns out this is true. Now the Nazis are moving you to the Stalag Luft I prison camp to avoid being overtaken by the Soviets.

Turn the page.

It's a long, cold march, and the guards have rifles trained on you the whole way. In spite of this, you and the other prisoners feel hopeful. If the Soviets are closing in, the war must be turning in the Allies' favor. You think the war might be over soon! But then a new fear takes hold. How will your captors treat you if they know they are going to lose? If they feel all is lost for them, they'll have little reason to treat you fairly. They may even torture or kill you.

You look around. Barren fields with no good places to hide stretch out on either side of the road. But up ahead, the road enters a wooded area. A person could hide in there. But without weapons or food, you will be at a disadvantage. It's probably smarter to wait and see what happens at the next camp. It all depends on how much you trust your captors.

To make a run for it, go to page 47.

To stay in line, turn to page 49.

As you enter the woods, you see a bend in the road ahead. You think there will be a few seconds when neither the guards in front nor the guards behind will have eyes on you. You breathe deeply to calm your rapid heartbeat. When you reach the bend, the guards ahead disappear from sight. Glancing back, you see only prisoners.

You dart to your right into the woods. You run about 40 feet and dive behind a fallen tree to wait.

Turn the page.

To your surprise, you don't hear anything. It seems no one noticed you run. You wait until the line of men disappears behind the bend, and then you get up and start running again.

Crack-crack-crack! The rapid report of a machine gun erupts from the road, and bullets split the bark in the trees ahead of you. You hit the dirt again to avoid getting shot, but you quickly realize you have little chance of escape. The smart thing to do is surrender and hope they don't kill you. But you could also keep running. Doing that would force the guards to chase you for a while. It could also slow down the march and give some of the other prisoners a chance to escape in the chaos.

To surrender, turn to page 51.

To keep running, turn to page 54.

You don't know how long you could last on your own out there even if you did get away. It is better to play it safe for now. If you stick with your fellow Kriegies, perhaps you can all reach freedom by working together.

After marching many days, you finally arrive at Stalag Luft I. You are among the first Americans to be housed at this prison camp. Prior to your arrival, it only held British prisoners.

You make friends with an officer of the Royal Air Force (RAF) named Chapman. He tells you that this used to be a pretty comfortable camp, but lately the conditions have been getting worse. That's because of all the additional Kriegies coming in from other camps. Rations have been reduced, and relief packages from the Red Cross and elsewhere have been blocked by the Germans.

Turn the page.

The more you learn about how badly the war is going for the Germans, the clearer it becomes that escape is critical. After all, the Germans—embarrassed by their impending defeat and facing future imprisonment for their war crimes—might start killing Kriegies whether you try to escape or not.

"I want to be on the escape committee," you tell Chapman. Every camp has one. Chapman smiles.

"What skills can you offer?" he asks.

Since your parents were German immigrants, you speak German. You can eavesdrop on German guards in hopes of learning information. Or you can tell the guards that you speak German and have conversations with them and try to learn information directly.

To eavesdrop, turn to page 55.

To engage directly with them, turn to page 58.

Slowly, with your hands high above your head, you stand up and face the road.

Your parents were German immigrants to America, so you grew up with that language. You use it now.

"I surrender!" you yell in German.

The guards approach, and one of them hits you in the face with the butt of his rifle. You crumple to the cold earth as more blows rain down. You cover your face with your arms as they finish their brutal assault.

The rest of the march to the new camp is even harder now. Not only are you bleeding from your head and mouth, but your left wrist is broken. You carry your bag with your right arm and cradle your left to your chest.

When you arrive at Stalag Luft I, you are thrown into a solitary cell. You are not given any medical treatment, and you lie on the floor in pain.

Turn the page.

Two weeks later, the guards let you out. You are weak and still bloody, but you are also angry. If you ever get the chance, you will make those Nazis pay.

Winter drags on, cold and miserable. Food, blankets, and clothing are sparse. Parcels of food, medicine, and books from the Red Cross—which used to come regularly—have stopped coming at all. Everyone is hungry, cold, and weak, and the camp gets increasingly crowded as more and more prisoners are transferred here. And one afternoon, the power goes out in camp when power lines are destroyed by battles in the region.

Meanwhile, someone with a secret radio has been listening to BBC news reports about the war and typing up stories to make an underground newspaper for prisoners. It's called the *POW WOW*, which stands for "Prisoners of War Waiting on Winning."

You learn two important details from the newspaper: The Soviets are closing in from the west, and the Americans are closing in from the east.

Clearly, the war will end very soon. Some prisoners are getting anxious. They want to escape now and make a break for the American line. They believe being rescued by the Soviets could delay their return home because leaders will need to sort through prisoner exchanges. Also, there are rumors the Soviet liberators may be volatile and dangerous. Even though the Soviets are your allies, you're not sure you can trust them.

As you lie in bed listening to the constant booming of not-so-distant artillery, you have a decision to make. Do you stay in the camp or try to make a break for the American line?

To stay in camp, turn to page 60.

To try to escape, turn to page 62.

You don't trust the Nazis to spare you even if you do surrender. If you're going to die anyway, you might as well try to help your fellow Kriegies. So, you jump up and run.

At first, no shots are fired. You run through the forest, crash through bushes, and trip over a root. As you get up, the shooting starts.

Bullets rip up the trees and splash the dirt around you. Then you feel something hard hit your back, and you stumble forward. You reach around, and your hand comes away slick with blood. You struggle to your feet and run again. But another shot hits your shoulder. You drop to your knees. You wish you'd been able to make the chase last a little longer. You only hope some of the other Kriegies got away in the chaos. But you will never know.

THE END

To follow another path, turn to page 11.
To learn more about Stalag Luft I, turn to page 101.

A watchtower and one of the barracks on the grounds of Stalag Luft I

You decide that you can learn more by eavesdropping. During recreational periods, you stake out a spot to do pushups and other exercises near the front gate where two guards are stationed. At night, you listen to the guards talk as they do security rounds of the barracks.

One night in bed, you hear the guards talking about some wires. You figure out that the Nazis have installed electrical wires beneath the barracks that detect vibrations. This means they'll be able to tell if anyone is digging—or tunneling—beneath the barracks.

Turn the page.

You report what you've heard to the senior Allied officer in camp, an American named Colonel Zemke. For now, he puts all efforts to escape on pause.

One day in April, the camp commandant orders Zemke to prepare the Kriegies to march out. The Soviets are coming, and you'll be moving to another camp. To your surprise, Zemke refuses.

"We are going nowhere," he says. Zemke tells him that the Germans may have guns, but the Kriegies have the numbers. He says you all will fight them rather than obey.

The commandant is surprised, and he leaves. A couple days pass. Then, on the morning of May 1, you wake up to find that there are no Germans in camp. They left overnight. Now Zemke is in charge of the camp. It is an astonishing turn of events.

The Red Army arrives the next day. Their leader meets with Zemke and lets him know that they plan to send all of you to the Soviet Union to await transportation home. For now, you are to wait.

Zemke has other ideas. He directs you and the other Kriegies to clear mines from a nearby airfield. He believes that Allied planes will come pick all of you up. He warns that waiting with the Soviets could lead to a months-long journey. You might even end up as pawns when the Soviet Union bargains with the U.S. and Britain about out how to divide things up after the war.

If Zemke is correct and planes do come, you want to be ready. But removing land mines from an airfield is dangerous work. Maybe you should refuse his order.

To work in the airfield clearing mines, turn to page 64.

To refuse the order, turn to page 67.

You figure you can learn more by talking to the guards than by eavesdropping. You befriend one guard in the mess hall. It turns out that your parents emigrated from his hometown, a suburb of Berlin. Over time, you convince him to sell you a sewing needle so you can mend some clothes for you and some of the other men. But really, you have other plans for the needle.

One of the Kriegies is able to magnetize it using a magnet he stole from a loudspeaker in camp. Then he sets it into a watch face so it can spin freely and act as a compass.

Meanwhile, another Kriegie has been able to create some forged identification papers. With the compass and the papers, you feel that you can make it to the line where the Americans are advancing.

One night in March, you and half a dozen other Kriegies crawl through a tunnel that's been dug from one of the barracks. When you emerge in the recreation field outside the camp, a blinding flashlight shines in your eyes. Then a growling dog latches onto your arm and pulls you from the hole. The pain is bad, but you fear it is only the beginning.

THE END

To follow another path, turn to page 11.
To learn more about Stalag Luft I, turn to page 101.

Why take any chances with the end so near? You may not totally trust the Soviets, but they are your allies. They will make sure you make it home—somehow.

So, you stay in camp and wait. One day, you wake up to find that the Nazis in charge of the camp have fled overnight. Now, the senior Allied officer, Colonel Zemke, is in charge. As the Soviets approach, you and all the prisoners put on armbands that say "American" or "English" in Russian so they won't mistakenly attack you.

The first group of Soviets come, and they are a ragtag group on horseback. Right away they tear down the barbed wire fences at camp. Many of them go into the nearby town of Barth and harass the local Germans. Some steal what they want, many get drunk, and others even shoot citizens.

While this is going on, Zemke orders the Kriegies to stay put and wait for an air rescue by the Americans. He is sure one must be coming. But some Kriegies are making a run for it.

Everything is chaotic right now, and it feels crazy to stay in this terrible camp one more day. Plus, there are rumors that the main Soviet army, when it comes, will make everyone go through Odessa in Ukraine before going home. That could take weeks.

That main Soviet force will arrive tomorrow, which means now might be your only chance to get away without going through Odessa. Other prisoners are already running.

To keep waiting, turn to page 69.

To leave, turn to page 71.

One night, as you lie in bed in your barracks, a Kriegie named Reese pulls a pair of wire cutters out of his mattress. He shows them in the moonlight streaming in the window and squeezes them a couple times.

"I stole them from the camp's shop," he whispers. "Snip-snip."

You understand immediately. He can cut the barbed wire that sits atop the fences surrounding camp.

"Let's do it," you say.

Several nights later, when the moon is just a sliver, you execute your plan. The two of you watch the guard patrolling the yard. As soon as he turns the corner of the building, you climb out your window and make a break for the fence.

Reese climbs up ahead of you and quickly snips the wires at the top. The wires spring open like a magic door.

In an instant, he is over the fence, working on cutting the coiled barbed wire in the space before the next fence. Soon, you are over the fence behind him.

"Stop right there!" says a voice in clumsy English. A searchlight illuminates the two of you. The guards force you to climb back inside the camp and put you in separate cells.

"Tomorrow," says the guard, "the Gestapo will be here. They will decide what to do with you. Ha ha ha ha ha!"

A tingle of terror runs up your spine. The Gestapo. You just hope they kill you quickly. The alternative is too awful to imagine.

THE END

To follow another path, turn to page 11.
To learn more about Stalag Luft I, turn to page 101.

You like Zemke, and you have quickly come to respect him as a leader. Besides, you'll do whatever it takes to help everyone get home.

"Yes, sir!" you say to Zemke. "Count me in!"

You and many other men begin the work of digging up mines from the nearby airfield. It feels amazing to be free outside the camp. It feels even more amazing to think about what lies ahead—going home! You are all very careful in your work. In a matter of days, you manage to clear all the mines on the air strip. If the planes come, they will be able to land here safely.

Finally, early one morning, a Red Army commander comes to camp to meet with Zemke. Afterward, Zemke tells you and the rest of the Kriegies to get your stuff together. You need to be ready to leave by 3:00 in the afternoon. You'll be flying out that day.

It's hard to believe. In fact, some of the men think it must be a trick. But you do as you are told and march out toward the airfield. As you get closer, you hear the heavy sound of large bombers—B-17s, also known as Flying Fortresses. Nobody doubts what is happening now. Those planes are coming for you!

When you arrive at the airfield, Allied officers are organizing everyone. Because you worked to clear the field, you get to board the first plane. As soon as it lands, you and dozens of others are hustled on board even as it is still rolling slowly along.

The scene is harried and rushed because they want to get everyone out as fast as possible—in case the plan changes and you have to go back. Even as you climb inside your plane, the next plane is already coming in for a landing.

Turn the page.

The bomber's interior has been cleared out—no bombs, no oxygen equipment, no seats. Everyone huddles against the side of the fuselage or grabs onto handles to stay as stable as they can. The door is slammed shut, and the bomber accelerates and lifts off the end of the runway. You can't see it, but you know the next bomber is already on the ground.

As the bomber flies low over the countryside, you look out the window. Farmland dotted with silos and buildings, forests, and soon the sea whips by. You shut your eyes and enjoy the ride.

THE END

To follow another path, turn to page 11.
To learn more about Stalag Luft I, turn to page 101.

You do not want to be killed by a mine just as the war has ended. Instead of marching with the other men to the airfield, you abandon them outside of camp and make your way to the town of Barth. The scene here is one of disarray. Many of the Soviet soldiers are stealing what they want, drinking in the bars, and fighting the locals. Some are even shooting civilians.

Present-day Barth, Germany

Turn the page.

You go to a tavern in hopes of getting a meal and a drink. Some Soviets are there bullying the woman behind the bar.

"Hey!" you call out in German, stepping into the fray. "Cut that out! The war is over, let's celebrate."

You had hoped that by speaking in German someone would have understood you. But you quickly realize that was a mistake. The Soviets don't understand you. Rather, they now think you are a German—their enemy—and they are angry you interrupted them. One of them points his gun at you. You close your eyes and await your fate.

THE END

To follow another path, turn to page 11.
To learn more about Stalag Luft I, turn to page 101.

You decide to wait. Even though the war is over, you don't have provisions or weapons, and you're not sure how well you would survive on your own.

The next morning, the main Soviet force arrives. Compared to the posse on horseback who arrived first, these men are cleaner, more orderly, and professional. Unfortunately, they are also adamant that all Allied POWs will be shipped through Odessa.

The Kriegies are very unhappy with the idea of a much longer journey home—or the idea of being under Soviet control for so long. Even though the Soviets are on your side, it is an uneasy alliance. After all, the Soviet Union is a communist country. Communism is a political system Western governments distrust and do not approve of.

Turn the page.

The Soviets do not allow the Kriegies to leave, and even though they treat you well, you begin to feel like hostages. One day, to feel better, you and the other Kriegies ceremoniously burn down the watch towers in camp. It is a joyous moment to watch those hated towers burn.

And then, on May 12, everything changes. It is announced that you'll be flying home. You don't know what changed, and you do not understand the negotiations that have transpired. And frankly, you don't care. All that matters is that you are going home. So, you pack your bag and get ready.

The next day, Mother's Day, you and hundreds of other men head to the airfield to await your flight.

THE END

To follow another path, turn to page 11.
To learn more about Stalag Luft I, turn to page 101.

By now you have been trapped behind barbed wire for two years. You're not going to wait one more day to be free. Also, many of the Soviets went into the town of Barth after they ordered the barbed wire fences torn down. You and many other Kriegies decide to join them.

In town, you befriend some of the Soviet soldiers. They buy you food and beverages as you celebrate together. Even the German tavern keeper seems to be having a good time.

During your two years in prison, you imagined being free again. But you never pictured yourself hanging out in a German tavern with Soviet roughnecks. It's not a bad ending, you decide. And it won't be long until the American troops reach town. You figure you can wait for them here.

THE END

To follow another path, turn to page 11.
To learn more about Stalag Luft I, turn to page 101.

Chapter 4

RESCUE MISSION

The war with Germany is all but over. Germany's leader, Adolf Hitler, killed himself a couple weeks ago on April 30. Then, on May 7, German General Alfred Jodl surrendered on behalf of his country. On May 8, people all over the world celebrated VE Day, or Victory in Europe Day. Five years of world war have left tens of millions of soldiers and civilians dead. About 6 million Jewish people have been systematically murdered by the Nazis. But now the European conflict that began in 1939 when Germany invaded Poland is finally over.

But the work is not complete. Allied forces still fight Japan in the Pacific. And Allied prisoners of war are still stuck in camps throughout Germany.

Turn the page.

НАШЕ ДЕЛО ПРАВОЕ. МЫ ПОБЕДИЛИ!

Пролетарии всех стран, соединяйтесь!

КОМСОМОЛЬСКАЯ ПРАВДА

Орган Центрального и Московского Комитетов ВЛКСМ

Четверг, 10 мая 1945 г. Цена 20 коп.

Великая Отечественная война завершилась нашей полной победой. Период войны в Европе кончился. Начался период мирного развития.

И. СТАЛИН.

Председатель Совета Народных Комиссаров СССР И. В. Сталин.

Премьер-министр Великобритании У. Черчилль.

Президент США Г. Трумэн.

Обращение тов. И. В. Сталина к народу

Товарищи! Соотечественники и соотечественницы!

Наступил великий день победы над Германией. Фашистская Германия, поставленная на колени Красной Армией и войсками наших союзников, признала себя побеждённой и об'явила безоговорочную капитуляцию.

7 мая был подписан в городе Реймсе предварительный протокол капитуляции. 8 мая представители немецкого главнокомандования в присутствии представителей Верховного Командования союзных войск и Верховного Главнокомандования советских войск подписали в Берлине окончательный акт капитуляции, исполнение которого началось с 24 часов 8 мая.

Зная волчью повадку немецких заправил, считающих договора и соглашения пустой бумажкой, мы не имеем оснований верить им на слово. Однако сегодня с утра немецкие войска во исполнение акта капитуляции

на алтарь отечества,— не прошли даром и увенчались полной победой над врагом. Вековая борьба славянских народов за своё существование и свою независимость окончилась победой над немецкими захватчиками и немецкой тиранией.

Отныне над Европой будет развеваться великое знамя свободы народов и мира между народами.

Три года назад Гитлер всенародно заявил, что в его задачи входит расчленение Советского Союза и отрыв от него Кавказа, Украины, Белоруссии, Прибалтики и других областей. Он прямо заявил: «Мы уничтожим Россию, чтобы она больше никогда не смогла подняться». Это было три года назад. Но сумасбродным идеям Гитлера не суждено было сбыться,—ход войны развеял их в прах. На деле получилось нечто прямо противоположное тому, о чём бредили гитлеровцы. Германия разбита наголову. Германские войска капитулируют. Советский Союз тор-

ПРИКАЗ
Верховного Главнокомандующего
ПО ВОЙСКАМ КРАСНОЙ АРМИИ И ВОЕННО-МОРСКОМУ ФЛОТУ

8 мая 1945 года в Берлине представителями германского верховного командования подписан акт о безоговорочной капитуляции германских вооружённых сил.

Великая Отечественная война, которую вёл советский народ против немецко-фашистских захватчиков, победоносно завершена, Германия полностью разгромлена.

Товарищи красноармейцы, краснофлотцы, сержанты, старшины, офицеры армии и флота, генералы, адмиралы и маршалы, поздравляю вас с победоносным завершением Великой Отечественной войны.

В ознаменование полной победы над Германией сегодня, 9 мая, в День Победы, в 22 часа столица нашей Родины Москва от имени Родины салютует доблестным войскам Красной Армии, кораблям и частям Военно-Морского Флота, одержавшим эту блестящую победу,— тридцатью артиллерийскими залпами из тысячи орудий.

Вечная слава героям, павшим в боях за свободу и независимость нашей Родины!

Да здравствуют победоносные Красная Армия и Военно-Морской Флот!

Верховный Главнокомандующий
Маршал Советского Союза И. СТАЛИН.

Front page of a Soviet newspaper from May 10, 1945, announcing victory over Nazi Germany and featuring (left to right) Soviet leader Joseph Stalin, British Prime Minister Winston Churchill, and U.S. President Harry S. Truman

Some of those prison camps, such as Stalag Luft I, have been liberated by Soviet forces. But the Soviets want to return the Allied POWs through the Black Sea port of Odessa, rather than through France.

Nobody in the British or American military likes that idea. For one, it would take too long to bring the POWs home. Also, the Soviets may be allies in the war, but they are not "friends."

Some worry the Soviets may use the POWs as bargaining chips to gain an advantage in the post-war world. Or worse, they might keep them for forced labor.

As an American officer, you have been following the situation on the ground in Germany. You learn that the Soviets are essentially holding the Allied prisoners hostage while their leader, Joseph Stalin, makes demands of the British and American leaders. You've heard that some POWs are breaking out of the camps to find a way home on their own—even when their own officers order them to stay.

You want to play a role in ending the chaos in Germany and getting the prisoners home.

To be a general involved in negotiations, turn to page 76.

To be a bomber pilot in England ready to fly into Germany, turn to page 79.

You are a general in the American Air Force. In the days after VE Day, you travel to Berlin with a group of Allied military and governmental personnel. You will meet with Soviet officials to discuss the POW situation. The Soviet group includes more than a dozen officers, including generals and dozens of armed bodyguards. American General Eisenhower sends a major general, and you rank just below him.

You, the major general, and a British general named Tailor sit at a long table with four Soviet generals. Each group also has a translator at the table. Behind the Soviets loom their bodyguards with guns and swords on their belts. The topic is how to get everyone's prisoners to their home countries, not only the Allied prisoners. There are Soviet prisoners all over Germany as well.

The U.S. major general starts things off. "I received a call from the ranking officer in Stalag Luft I describing a chaotic and dangerous situation," he says. "We will fly in and take our men out tomorrow."

The Soviet translator relays your message to the Soviet generals. They talk amongst themselves. Then one of them speaks, and your translator explains that the Soviets consider Stalag Luft I to be their territory now. Stalin has given orders for British and American POWs to come out over land to Odessa.

"Many of our men are sick," Tailor says. "We want them home."

The Soviets then change the subject. They want their prisoners back quickly because they believe many of these soldiers defected and fought on the side of Germany. Stalin considers them enemies and will punish them.

Turn the page.

In fact, Stalin sees anyone who was captured alive as an enemy of the Soviet Union. For that reason, many Soviet prisoners want to go to America.

The major general turns to you. You've been on the ground here for a long time, and he trusts your opinion. Should you give up the Soviet prisoners, putting them at risk of being executed when they get home? That might allow you to get your own men out of Germany through France. But the thought of sending all those Soviets to their deaths is hard to swallow.

To suggest offering up the Soviet POWs, turn to page 81.

To try another tactic, turn to page 83.

You are an American bomber pilot in England. Now that the Allies have defeated Germany, you and the other men on your base are worried about how Allied POWs will be treated before they can be rescued. You have seen men do terrible things during the war, and you know that the Nazis certainly have no love for Americans. The best thing is to get those prisoners out as quickly as possible.

B-17 bomber pilot and copilot (back row right) with their crew in England

Turn the page.

One morning, you are called in for a briefing.

"Men," your commander says, "today we have an important unarmed mission."

As he explains that you will fly low over northern Germany, your mind begins calculating the risks. Since Germany has surrendered, no one should be shooting at you. But word travels slowly, and you aren't sure fighters everywhere in the country have received the news. Will you really be safe? Even though the war is over, will angry Nazis resist the urge to fire on a low-flying bomber?

"We only need one plane for now," your commander says at the end of his briefing.

There are two crews here, so you could stay back where it's safe. On the other hand, he said the mission is important.

To take the assignment, turn to page 85.

To stay back in the hangar, turn to page 87.

"Give them their men," you say. "We get our men. Fair swap. We can't control what happens after that. It's not our business."

The major general looks over at the cadre of armed Soviet bodyguards, as if imagining the violent fate that likely awaits the Soviet prisoners. Finally, he looks at Tailor, then at you, and nods in agreement. The most important thing is to get the American and British men home as quickly and as safely as possible.

"Those Soviets might be killed or sent to the Gulag when they get back home," he says, "but the well-being of our men is more important."

You tell the Soviet generals, and one of them leaves to make a phone call—presumably to Stalin to get permission. When he comes back, he confers briefly with the other generals and says you have a deal.

Turn the page.

A group of Allied airmen at Stalag Luft I

You leave the meeting in good spirits, but a few days later there is a new sticking point. The Soviets have released prisoners from several camps, but they are still holding the prisoners at Stalag Luft I. That camp currently has more than 9,000 prisoners, and the Soviets aren't budging. Should you try to force an air rescue, risking a fight with Stalin? Or do you negotiate to find out what the new issue is?

To try to evacuate without permission from the Soviets, turn to page 90.

To negotiate with the Soviets first, turn to page 92.

"We can't send those men to their deaths," you say. "We don't know if they betrayed the Allies or not. But Stalin will not wait to find out. He will kill them all or imprison them in a Gulag."

The major general doesn't respond at first—he's thinking. Tailor, the British general, speaks up.

"I am not sure I agree," he says.

"I am sure," the major general says while staring into your eyes, "that our men are more important than theirs. I am sure that you have misplaced your patriotism."

He tells you not to speak again for the rest of the negotiations.

To Tailor, he says, "We need to get our men home as soon and as safely as possible. I am going to offer them their prisoners. Do you agree?"

Turn the page.

"I do," says Tailor.

You sit silently as the other men at the table talk. In the end, the swap is made. What will happen to you after giving the wrong advice during such an important negotiation remains to be seen. If the major general is as angry as he seems, he could destroy your career with the snap of his fingers.

THE END

To follow another path, turn to page 11.
To learn more about Stalag Luft I, turn to page 101.

You've heard that the German generals are unpredictable. If they decide to take revenge on the Allies, the prisoners in those camps are like fish in a barrel. You will do anything to help get them out. You take the mission.

Your job is to fly over towns and prison camps while dropping leaflets written in German. The leaflets contain a warning: Treat Allied personnel humanely or the Americans will come for you and make you pay.

A British airman loads leaflets into a chute to be dropped over German-held territories.

Turn the page.

You fly your bomber low. Over Barth, the bomb bay opens and leaflets flutter out.

You continue on to Stalag Luft I and repeat the process. The leaflets spin and fall like big snowflakes. Nobody shoots at you.

With your mission completed, you return to the air base in France. As you walk across the tarmac to the briefing area, your commander meets you at the door. You salute him, and he congratulates you on completing an important mission.

"I have two more assignments," he says. Then he explains how you can be part of a group that flies to an airfield near Barth and prepares the runway for the rescue operation. Or you can pilot one of the rescue planes.

To fly to an airfield near Barth, turn to page 94.

To pilot one of the rescue planes, turn to page 97.

"I'll stay back this time," you say. It might not be the bravest choice, but this has been a long war, and you don't want to get shot down now that it's over.

"Fine," the commander says coldly. "You're dismissed."

Later, the commander calls you back to the room.

"Get your B-17 bomber ready for an operation," he says. He wants you and your crew to remove everything from the inside—bombing apparatus, oxygen equipment, seats, everything. "It needs to be light and nimble so it can carry as many of our boys as possible."

The rest of the afternoon, you and your crew work on stripping the plane. You work in silence, and you can tell your men wish they were flying on a mission instead. They would feel like they were doing more good that way.

Turn the page.

A B-17 bomber crew near their plane after returning from a mission

Finally, the other bomber returns from its mission. Turns out it dropped leaflets over German towns and prison camps warning the Germans to treat the Allied prisoners well.

The next afternoon, your bomber is all fueled up and ready for a mission. Word is out that it will be used to rescue men who have been held at Stalag Luft I! You can't wait to see the looks on their faces as you tell them they're going home. You put on your helmet and start walking toward your plane when the commander yells your name.

"Yes, sir?" you say, turning around.

"You're out. Detlef will be flying your plane today."

"Sir?"

"You're not flying," he says.

Then a pilot named Detlef climbs into the cockpit of your plane. You watch as your bomber lumbers toward the runway.

You suppose this is your commander's way of punishing you for opting out of the leaflet job. It breaks your heart to miss the rescue, but you'll just have to hear about it later.

THE END

To follow another path, turn to page 11.
To learn more about Stalag Luft I, turn to page 101.

The major general calls you to discuss the situation.

"To heck with the Soviets," you say over the phone. "They went back on their word. Let's go get our boys—what are they going to do about it?"

The major general hangs up, and you start preparing a mission to fly in and get the men at Stalag Luft I. You'll come in armed, and you'll fight if necessary.

But before you can implement the plan, you get another phone call, this one from the major general's secretary.

"Your orders are to wait," he says.

"We look weak if we wait," you say.

"You have your orders," the secretary says. "We do not want to make the Reds angry now."

"May I speak to the major general?" you ask.

"He will not be taking your calls," the secretary says.

You realize that the major general thinks your advice was so bad that he can't trust you anymore. You are not included in further negotiations. And when the rescue operation finally happens, you are not a part of it.

THE END

To follow another path, turn to page 11.
To learn more about Stalag Luft I, turn to page 101.

"Let's see what they want," you suggest to the major general when he calls to discuss the situation. "No need to risk the safety of our men when we're so close."

"I agree," he says.

Another meeting is arranged. Once again, you sit at the table with the Soviet generals who are backed by heavily armed guards. You start the discussion.

"The agreement was for a swap," you say. "You've gone back on your word."

"That was before we heard about Vlasov," one of the Soviets responds.

You know who he's talking about. Your troops captured Soviet General Andrey Vlasov and are holding him in Germany. He had previously been captured by the Germans and defected to their side. He raised an army of 50,000 German-captured Soviets and trained them to fight on the side of the Nazis.

You suspect that Stalin badly wants to get his hands on this high-profile traitor. And once he does, he'll likely have him killed.

Unlike the other Soviet prisoners, you have no second thoughts about turning over Vlasov. After all, his army killed many Allies, including your own men. You explain the situation to the major general.

"Give them the traitor," he says.

"If you can guarantee the safe and rapid air rescue of the prisoners at Stalag Luft I, Vlasov is yours," you tell the Soviets.

They quickly agree. You make a phone call to the Allied officers in Stalag Luft I and tell them to pack their bags. They'll be flying out tomorrow.

THE END

To follow another path, turn to page 11.
To learn more about Stalag Luft I, turn to page 101.

Preparing a landing strip is less glorious than conducting a rescue, but you will be there as the prisoners arrive at the airfield and the first rescue planes come in. You'll get to congratulate and celebrate with some of the prisoners.

Before you leave the base, you learn of a surprise. General Bill Gross, commander of the 1st Combat Wing, is in charge of the operation and will be flying with you. You salute him as he approaches the plane.

Brigadier General Bill Gross (right) awarding an airman in 1945

"It's an honor, sir," you tell him.

The flight to Barth is bumpy, but your landing is smooth. You taxi your B-17 to the end of the field. Then you and your crew unload wood, tools, and other supplies to build a radio tower. This tower will be used to receive and dispatch rescue planes virtually nonstop until all the Stalag Luft I prisoners are out of Germany.

The tower is barely complete before you hear the sound of the rumbling bombers approaching the field. At this point, however, the planes don't have permission to land. You know that negotiations to get permission from the Soviets to fly out the Allied POWs have been ongoing. But you don't know what the holdup is.

Then, suddenly, General Gross takes a short phone call. When he hangs up, he turns to you.

Turn the page.

“The boys are going home,” he says.

Before long, dozens of men arrive at the field. Most look ragged, thin, and exhausted. Many have been in the camp for years. But many are smiling, eyes wide with excitement. As the first bomber comes in for a landing, one prisoner bursts out laughing. Even General Gross is smiling.

While the first plane lands, you greet prisoners and check their names against a shipping roster. You organize them into the groups and shake their hands as you direct them into the airplane.

When the first plane takes off with its cargo of free men, you and everyone else on the ground let out a great cheer. It feels like the war is finally and truly over.

THE END

To follow another path, turn to page 11.
To learn more about Stalag Luft I, turn to page 101.

With fellow Americans stuck in a hostile place, your only desire is to get them out. So, you take the rescue mission. Your plane will be among the first group to fly in.

You climb into the B-17 bomber, and your stomach tingles with butterflies as you accelerate down the runway and lift into the air. You fly low, looking out over the German cities and fields that you had bombed in previous runs. No one is shooting anti-aircraft guns at you now. There is little chatter on the radio. It feels strangely calm after the frenzy of combat.

When you reach the airfield, you circle until permission is granted to land. At the landing strip below, you can see soldiers looking up, waiting. They are the men who set up the airfield for the rescue operation. But so far, you don't see any prisoners.

Turn the page.

Then, suddenly, you see them marching on a road. The all-clear call to land comes in over the radio!

You bank one last time and direct your plane toward the runway. You land and, according to your orders, taxi toward the waiting men. An officer on the ground directs a group of prisoners into the plane, and within just a few minutes, you lift off into the air again.

A B-17 Flying Fortress

Your copilot goes back with the prisoners, all of whom were airmen. Several of the men are hugging one another. Someone is weeping.

You fly low, skimming trees and towns to give everyone a show. The mood becomes quiet in the back as everyone simply takes in the moment. It is a moment you will never forget.

THE END

To follow another path, turn to page 11.
To learn more about Stalag Luft I, turn to page 101.

Chapter 5

THE LIBERATION OF STALAG LUFT I

Stalag Luft I was right outside the German seaside city of Barth. It was originally opened to hold British airmen, but Americans started being transferred there in 1943. The prisoners called themselves "Kriegies." It was short for the German word *Kriegsgefangener*, which means "prisoner of war."

Early on, Stalag Luft I had a reputation for having decent living conditions for a prison camp. But by late 1944, its conditions were quickly getting worse. With Germany losing ground in the war, food became more scarce as the Germans cut off delivery of Red Cross packages. Water and electric power went out periodically as battles raged in the region.

Allied prisoners in a cramped hospital of a liberated German POW camp

Meanwhile, POWs were weak and demoralized. In January and February 1945, other German camps closed as the Soviet Red Army advanced. Prisoners from those camps were marched hundreds of miles to Stalag Luft I, which became overcrowded.

By April 1945, the Red Army was nearing Stalag Luft I. Rumors began to circulate among the prisoners that the Germans knew they were going to lose the war.

The German commandant of the camp, Oberst von Warnstedt, told the top Allied officer in camp, Colonel Hubert Zemke, that the Kriegies would be marching to another camp. But Zemke knew he had the advantage. He refused Warnstedt's order because he had way more men than the commandant and the Red Army was closing in. Instead, Zemke negotiated a peaceful transfer of power for the camp, and the Germans evacuated overnight.

When the Kriegies woke up that morning, they had no captors. Colonel Zemke was in charge of the camp.

When the first Red Army soldiers arrived at Stalag Luft I, the prisoners all put on armbands identifying themselves as American or British soldiers. The Soviets ordered the barbed wire to be torn down, and Zemke ordered all the Kriegies to stay put and wait for rescue by American planes.

But the situation in camp and in Barth soon grew hectic. Many of the Soviet troops terrorized the town and, despite orders, many Kriegies joined them. Several hundred others simply left with hopes of walking to the advancing Allied line and going home that way. After months or years in camp, they couldn't wait another day. To maintain order and keep as many Kriegies in camp as possible, Zemke established a military police force.

Meanwhile, the Allies were negotiating an air rescue of the Kriegies behind the scenes. Zemke and the senior British officer in camp identified a nearby airfield that could be used for a rescue. They reported this to the Allied officers holding negotiations and sent Kriegies out to clear the field of mines and debris. Finally, word came that they would soon be flying out.

Several B-17 bombers flying in formation

The planes came in with less than two minutes between them. The pilots didn't even turn off their engines as the POWs were quickly loaded and they took off again. The mission, "Operation Revival," involved more than 450 separate bomber flights. It succeeded in rescuing nearly 9,000 prisoners.

MORE ABOUT OPERATION REVIVAL

- ››› Roughly 94,000 Americans were held captive in European prison camps during World War II. By the end of the war, 7,717 of them were in Stalag Luft I. About 1,400 British prisoners were also held captive there when the war ended.

- ››› Before being captured, Colonel Hubert Zemke commanded the 56th Fighter Group, also known as "Zemke's Wolfpack." He was shot down on October 30, 1944, after 154 missions. He arrived at Stalag Luft I in December of that year.

- ››› Many prisoners at Stalag Luft I had heard rumors that the Soviets wanted to ship them home by way of Odessa, a Soviet port in southern Ukraine more than 1,200 miles (1,930 kilometers) away. This route was not only much longer than going home through France, but it was also worrisome. The Americans and British didn't fully trust the Soviets. As one POW wrote years later, they considered the Soviets "Allies" but not "friends."

- ››› Historians believe a captured Soviet general was a key to the negotiations to conduct the Stalag Luft I rescue. The Americans had caught General Andrey Vlasov and were holding him in Germany. Vlasov defected to Germany and raised an army of 50,000 Soviet POWs to fight against the Soviet Union. Soviet leader Joseph Stalin badly wanted that general, so that he could exact revenge. When the Americans offered him up, the air rescue was given the green light.

››› An advance team from England flew to an airfield near Stalag Luft I before the air rescue. American General Bill Gross was in charge of the operation. His mission was to prepare the airfield for the rescue, build a radio tower, and establish POW shipping rosters for each plane.

››› On May 12, 1945, the first B-17s flew to Barth to pick up prisoners. They flew under 10,000 feet (3,050 meters) because they had been stripped of oxygen equipment, weapons, and other gear in order to make room for more passengers and keep the plane light. Instead of flying with the usual crew of 10, they flew with just a pilot, copilot, navigator, radio man, and flight engineer.

A ten-member crew poses by their B-17 bomber at a British airfield in 1944.

THE B-17 BOMBER

The B-17 Flying Fortress was one of the most iconic aircraft of World War II. This American heavy bomber had four engines and was often used to fly high above enemy territory while conducting daytime bombing runs. By flying at 25,000 to 35,000 feet (7,600 to 10,600 meters), they could often avoid the range of German anti-aircraft fire. All told, around 12,730 B-17s were built between 1936 and 1945.

The B-17 Memphis Belle

Inside an equipped B-17

For Operation Revival, B-17s were stripped down to make them lighter and allow them to rescue as many soldiers as possible. All unnecessaryequipment was removed, including oxygen apparatus and weapons.

TIMELINE

1940—Stalag Luft I is opened near the seaside town of Barth to hold British officers.

APRIL 1942—The camp is closed and prisoners are transferred to other camps.

OCTOBER 1942—The camp is reopened for British airmen.

1943—American POWs start being held there.

DECEMBER 1944—Colonel Hubert Zemke arrives in camp.

JANUARY 1945—German power lines are destroyed, cutting off electricity in camp; many new prisoners arrive in camp after being evacuated from other camps and marched hundreds of miles in subzero temperatures; the camp becomes overcrowded.

FEBRUARY 1945—The Germans cut off Red Cross parcels to the prisoners, which had helped supplement the meager food the camp provided; the prisoners begin to starve.

APRIL 1945—Conditions start to get better as the Germans realize they are going to lose the war; Red Cross parcels are delivered again; the Germans even salute Colonel Zemke.

LATE APRIL—The German commandant tries to order an evacuation, but Zemke refuses.

APRIL 30—The Germans leave camp in the middle of the night.

MAY 1—The first group of Soviet troops arrives.

MAY 2—More Soviets arrive, taking control of the camp.

MAY 8—Victory in Europe Day is celebrated.

MAY 12—The first planes arrive to evacuate men to France.

MAY 15—The final evacuations take place.

GLOSSARY

airman (AYR-man)—a military pilot, aviator, or aviation technician

barracks (BAR-uhks)—a building where prisoners are housed

commandant (COM-uhn-dawnt)—commanding officer

communism (KAHM-yuh-ni-zuhm)—a system in which goods and property are owned by the government and shared in common; communist rulers limit personal freedoms to achieve their goals

contraband (KAHN-truh-band)—items that are not allowed in prisons

dinghy (DING-ee)—a small open boat

Gulag (GOO-lahg)—a Soviet labor camp

hangar (HANG-ur)—a large building where aircraft are housed and repaired

hostage (HOSS-tij)—a person held against his or her will

incinerator (in-SIN-uh-ray-tur)—a furnace for burning waste materials at very high temperatures

negotiate (ni-GOH-shee-ate)—to bargain or discuss something to come to an agreement

solitary confinement (SOL-uh-ter-ee kuhn-FINE-muhnt)—a punishment in which a prisoner is put in a cell alone and not allowed to see or talk to anyone

squadron (SKWAHD-ruhn)—a unit of the military

SS (ESS-ESS)—a Nazi paramilitary unit used to cruelly enforce intelligence, security, policing, and mass exterminations

READ MORE

Doeden, Matt. *Can You Survive a World War II Escape?: An Interactive History Adventure.* North Mankato, MN: Capstone Press, 2024.

Havemeyer, Janie. *World War II in Europe.* Minneapolis: Core Library, 2025.

Monroe, Alex. *World War II.* Minneapolis: Bellwether Media, Inc., 2024.

INTERNET SITES

Ducksters: World War II
ducksters.com/history/world_war_ii

The National WWII Museum: Operation Revival: Rescue from Stalag Luft I
nationalww2museum.org/war/articles/operation-revival-stalag-luft-i

U.S. Department of Defense: Victory in Europe Day
defense.gov/Multimedia/Experience/VE-Day

ABOUT THE AUTHOR

Eric Braun is a children's author and editor. He has written dozens of books on many topics. One of his books was even read by an astronaut on the International Space Station for kids on Earth to watch. Eric lives in Minneapolis, Minnesota, where you can usually find him on his bike.

MORE BOOKS IN THIS SERIES

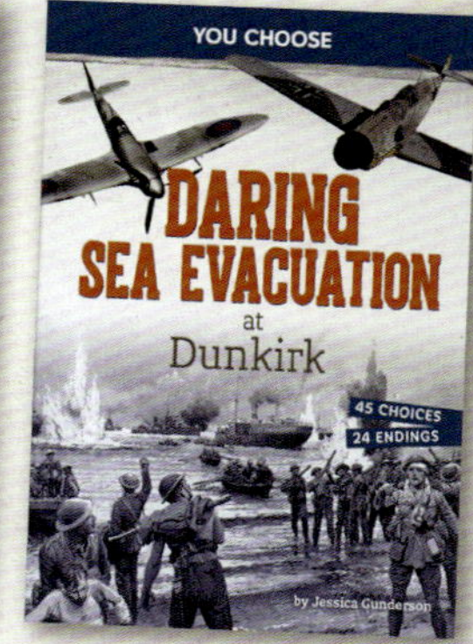